Grace Under Fire: One Marine's Journey

C. Ben Barbour (USMC)

DEDICATION

To the father I never knew but the person I always loved; the mother who was the toughest person I've ever met — my respect for her has no boundaries; the sister I have watched mature in the Christian faith while battling breast cancer for 6 years; and the brother who was too good for this world. He died from an aneurysm at age 21 and I will always regret not knowing him better.

"The invisible presence of these blessed spirits is of great help and comfort to us. They walk alongside us and protect us in every circumstance, they defend us from dangers and we can turn to them at every moment."

&Pope Benedict XVI
September 29, 2008

"It is not the army of lions led by a sheep that frightens me – but rather , the army of sheep led by a lion."

&Alexander the Great

CONTENTS

ACKNOWLEDGMENTS

Many thanks to my sister Becky for bugging me over the years to write my story down on paper. Thanks also to my minister John "Randy" Riddle who finally convinced me to start writing. Also, to my research and administrative team, Libby Clarkson and Dawn Meehan. Thank you all!

FOREWORD

Vietnam

"I waited and watched those Marines about to go into battle. Some were standing watch, some readied equipment, and some slept or rested, but all were quiet. No nervous jabbering, no false bravado, no whining, no melodrama...they were professionals. Most were teenagers; many far less than a year away from home, but they were seasoned by months of fighting with a determined enemy. Despite their youth and their relatively short time in the Corps, they were as willing and professional as anyone whoever wore a uniform. I was proud to be among them."

                                ❧ Lt. Vic Taylor, USMC

                   From The Magnificent Bastards, by Keith Nolan

1
SEEKING FORGIVENESS AT 34,000 FEET

"Blessed is he whose transgression is
forgiven, whose sin is covered."
(Psalm 32:1)

April 1968

Looking out the window I again was amazed at how peaceful everything below the plane appeared from five miles over the South China Sea. Our planeload of Marines was about ninety minutes from our departure point at Kadena Air Force base in Okinawa and we were about an hour from our destination of Da Nang, South Vietnam. The flight was smooth and characterized by a minimum of nervous conversation.

The Continental flight attendants worked with a professional demeanor and tried to keep their conversations with the Marines light-hearted and non-intrusive. However, no amount of professional training could disguise the nervousness and pity in their eyes. Everybody on that flight knew what the reality was – within six weeks of joining their units, some of these Marines would be wounded or dead. The war in Vietnam was heating up at a fast pace.

Four months earlier both the American and South Vietnam governments and military were taken by surprise when the North Vietnam government launched a countrywide offensive against South Vietnam and the multi-national forces engaged in the fighting. The surprising attack came to be designated the "Tet Offensive" and it raised the ferocity of fighting exponentially.

As the plane continued towards Da Nang, my inner feelings, as well as my stomach, were surprisingly calm. For some reason unknown to me, I felt at peace.

While stationed in Okinawa and awaiting this flight, I had on several occasions watched caravans of military trucks filled to capacity with helmets, flak jackets, clothing and other personal gear all caked in various shades of mud. When I asked where all this equipment came from, I was informed that they were all personal effects from the fighting at a large northernmost United States firebase known as Khe Sanh. This base contained thousands of Marine and Naval personnel, many artillery batteries, and a landing zone large enough for both helicopter units and fixed wing aircraft as well as a hospital. It was then that I realized that all those trucks were bringing back the personal effects of the wounded and killed from Khe Sanh. More than anything else, that experience in Okinawa brought home the reality of what I was flying into.

Therefore, with about an hour remaining until we

touched down in Da Nang, I decided this might be my last chance to communicate with my mom in a safe environment. I felt the need to ask her forgiveness for doing really dumb things. At the age of nineteen I had made more than my share of "bad" choices.

For this chapter and indeed the book itself to make sense, I feel the need to trace a little of my family's background.

My dad died in 1953 at Duke Hospital in Durham, North Carolina. He was thirty-one years old and left behind my mother, younger sister Becky (age four), younger brother David (age two), and myself, the oldest at age six. Within three years of dad's death, the doctors discovered a lump on mom's left arm, which was soon diagnosed as cancer, and her arm was amputated at the elbow. Within a year of this, mom's dad died as well. So in the late 1950's, mom became a single parent with three young children, a left arm replaced by a prosthesis, working as a secretary at a lumber mill owned and run by some of her cousins.

To this day, I have never met a stronger or more determined individual. As with all mothers, she worried about her children and was the proto-typical strong southern lady. In the end, all three of us kids had a college education and a strict upbringing. There was never too much money but we never lacked for the essentials.

The Church was the cornerstone around which

everything rotated. There was more than one time that I felt maybe we should just all move in there. I was in the choir, young people's group, Boy Scouts, and an acolyte at Sunday Church services.

When I was in the tenth grade, Mother moved us from North Carolina to the town she grew up in located in the mid-western part of South Carolina. The move was motivated probably for numerous reasons but mainly, we kids were growing up and she felt the need to re-locate back to her roots to get some assistance from her immediate family (eventually the three children became two)

A couple of years after my return from Vietnam, my brother, David, died instantly from a thoracic aneurysm. David had been diagnosed earlier in his life as a child with Marfan syndrome. A condition characterized by being very tall, very thin, double jointed just about everywhere, and with very poor vision. Everything inside his body was slightly off-kilter. His heart was in the wrong place and as a child he was plagued by delayed language development. Mom used to take him to Fort Bragg near Fayetteville so he could receive speech and language therapy.

David was a senior in college, just a few months short of graduating, when he was taken to the emergency room with mom by his side. David's aorta burst just as the doctor was finding a gurney for him. His death was instantaneous. Mom must have known that David would probably not live a normal life span, but after everything she had gone through, I began to have dialogues with God about the unfairness of it all. (This line of thought will be picked up later in the book regarding Post Traumatic Stress Disorder.)

Mother died over a decade ago. She passed peacefully in a hospital with my sister Becky in attendance. I arrived shortly thereafter. She had died but her presence was still in the room. I knew she was lingering long enough for me to be with her. I told her that I would miss her; I loved her and was so happy she, dad and my brother were together again.

Now back on the plane, Da Nang is getting closer and I need to close this letter to the person for whom I have the greatest respect and love. The letter was primarily a way to let her know how I felt about her as a mom and an unbelievably tough human being. I apologized for all the times I know I hurt her by stupid decisions and actions on my part. I told her of my love and admiration for her as a human being and a mother. I told her that no matter what happened in the next thirteen-month tour of duty, I promised to make her proud and I would try every day to be the "meanest mother in the valley."

Author's Note:

Two and a half weeks after I joined my unit on April 13, 1968, Mom received a letter from the US State Department regretting to inform her that, "your son is missing in action". More details about that in Chapter 5.

2
YOUR NEW BEST FRIEND IS A WHAT?

"My God sent His angel and shut the lions'
mouths so that they have not hurt me..."
(Daniel 6:22)

It was now early summer 1968 and our unit had been moved from the coastal region into the central highlands of South Vietnam. The company, "Golf", was located on top of a ridge connecting two mountaintops. (At an earlier time, our accommodations belonged to the North Vietnamese army. The site had long been abandoned so we moved right in.)

Summer had arrived and it was hot, but still not as hot as the coastal plain had been. Normally, the company did not stay anywhere more than a week or two. We were between operations as the fighting had calmed down. Two nights earlier we had taken mortar fire from the surrounding mountains but luckily no one was wounded or killed.

Our daily routine consisted of one patrol sent off in the morning and one patrol sent in the afternoon. These patrols usually consisted of a ten to twelve man squad. The squads rotated the patrols so we averaged two patrols per week. The objective of all patrols was to find and engage the North Vietnamese troops that we knew were in the area.

At night, every night, we also sent out ambush teams to engage North Vietnamese troops who took too much interest in us. We had access to starlight scopes that allowed us to "see in the dark" although the light was actually green.

On a Wednesday in early June, it was our squad's turn in the rotation for afternoon patrol. A typical patrol was out for about three to five hours depending on the terrain. Our squad leader's last name was Davis. He was a sergeant from Florida who loved country music, especially "Buck Owens and the Buckaroos", and he would sing, "I have a tiger by the tail – it's plain to see." Little did he know that the song would soon be prophetic.

We left camp around one in the afternoon with a squad of eight men. Sergeant Davis was the squad leader and we hoped he knew where we were supposed to go. Reading topographical maps in an unknown place can be dicey at best. For some reason, on this patrol, Sergeant Davis decided that I should walk "the point". This was something I had done many times but I never liked it. Whoever was walking point had the responsibility to make sure the patrol did not walk into an ambush. Therefore, I walked about twenty to thirty meters in advance of the rest of the patrol.

My job was to be alert for "booby traps" and any enemy activity. It was also quite likely that if we got in a fight, I would probably be the first killed. Oddly enough, over time, you make peace with that reality and do not worry too much about it.

We had been out of camp for about three hours when Sergeant Davis called for a stop and rest. We had covered several miles and it was steamy, humid, and hot. The terrain was mountainous and thick with vegetation. We had seen no indication of North Vietnamese activity but we knew they were in the area. The enemy knew from experience that Marines loved to pick a fight, so we rarely just bumped into them unless they thought they had the advantage.

After about ten or fifteen minutes, we "saddled up" and continued. We reached an area that was dense with elephant grass. This grass was thick and grew to a height of about four to five feet; a great place for an ambush. I slowed everybody down so I could move a little slower and quieter. The squad was still about thirty meters behind me when I saw something strange. About thirty meters in front of me, the grass was deliberately bent over at a forty-five degree angle. It provided shade and some protection from the daily afternoon rain shower. I held up my arm silently. This, in a nonverbal way, told the squad leader to halt the patrol.

My first thought was that I had run up on an observation position where there would be one or two

North Vietnamese forward artillery observers. Their job was to scout out truck caravans carrying equipment and supplies for our troops. Then they would radio the position coordinates for the convoys. Soon after that, the big guns from the north would open fire and create havoc for the convoys.

I signaled for the patrol to stop and spread out in case this developed into a fight. The way the grass was deliberately shaped to provide relief from the sun as well as cover from any American helicopters flying overhead led me to firmly believe that we had walked straight up to a forward observation point. I flicked the safety off on my rifle and moved as quietly and slowly as possible.

Coming from the rear of the "lean-to", I slowly advanced closer and closer. I was convinced we had accidentally caught these guys in the open and if we could surprise them this fight would not last long. I moved closer, until I could just barely peep around the corner of their position. I was looking for one or two humans with brown eyes. Instead, I found myself looking into a single set of large green eyes.

This picture was not computing! I continued to stare – looking for men. I finally realized that I was looking at something else. The green eyes belonged to a huge head, and the huge head belonged to a huge body - a good nine to ten feet long. The huge body belonged to one of the famous Bengal tigers of Vietnam and I had just walked right up on it. I had heard stories of these tigers since I arrived but never thought much about it. I could feel the tension building in me and the patrol behind me, but I was not able to take my eyes off what I had stumbled onto.

It became obvious that if that tiger was hungry, I would be a nice afternoon snack. However, the tiger seemed quite content sunning itself in the afternoon sun. I knew that if it decided to charge from such a short distance I would not stand a chance of surviving the encounter. The thought crossed my mind that this cat would be on me before I could pull the trigger. I decided that if I fired my rifle it would only irritate this beast. In addition, if it jumped on me, the weight alone would have killed me.

It was at this pivotal point that I suddenly calmed down. Somehow, I was in the "presence" of somebody else. This "presence" told me calmly <u>not</u> to shoot the tiger and instead move slowly back to the squad. There was also an explanation – "The tiger has already eaten and is sleepy in the sun." I cannot explain the communication beyond saying that the message to me was accompanied by an otherworldly sense of calm and well-being.

I moved ever so slowly backward while the tiger continued to watch me. I finally got back to Sergeant Davis and told him what was lying in front of us. He was obviously not convinced so he went storming up in the tiger's direction. I watched him come to an abrupt stop then slowly back off and return to us. For a Florida boy who usually was very suntanned, Sergeant Davis was now as white as a ghost! He called back to the company captain and explained the situation. The captain finally agreed to a change of course and we proceeded on a new path.

Postscript:

About two hours after the tiger encounter, the company captain called back to see if we could re-trace our route and find the tiger. He had thought about it and decided that we should go find the tiger, kill it, and bring it back to him. He thought a tiger rug would look good in his den back home in the States. We assured him that we could not find the tiger again since we were two hours away from that position. Also, since then we had accidentally kicked over a honeybee nest and most of the squad had multiple stings as a result.

Moreover, since we had had to divert from our original course, there was no way we would have time to retrace our route and get back before dark. In enemy territory, you do not want to be fumbling in the dark - bumping into every other tree. We did finally get back to our company and not a single soul would believe the story of the tiger.

I personally said a long prayer of thanks, not just regarding the tiger, but also more importantly, for the spiritual Providential communication of which there would be more to come soon.[1]

The encounter with the "Presence" as introduced in this chapter is one of several such encounters detailed in this book. While it is plausible that the "Presence" was a messenger angel sent to give instructions to me while in a tight situation, the term "Presence" seems to best describe in human terms what was happening.

The communication from the "Presence" to me regarding remaining "calm" was not heard – but rather, it was "felt." The "voice" was neither male nor female but the message was perfectly clear and in the English language. From a practical point of view, simply the nearness of this being brought instant calmness and a total absence of fear.

My sister has an interesting hypothesis regarding the tiger encounter. She suggested that like Daniel in the Lions Den (Book of Daniel – chapter 6), maybe the tiger could see the "Presence" with me. Can animals "see" spiritual beings? – I do not know but it is an interesting proposal.

---

[1] This hearing a Voice in combat is not without precedent. I refer to E.B. Sledge's experience of "hearing a voice" in With the Old Breed: At Peleliu and Okinawa, pg. 99. (Sledge, 1981)

3
FROM THE BEST TO THE VERY, VERY WORST

"... you do not know what will happen tomorrow. For what is your life? It is even a vapor that appears for a little time and then vanishes away. Instead you ought to say, "If the Lord wills, we shall live and do this or that." (James 4:13-15)

Summer 1968 (I-Corps)

Another operation in a seemingly endless number of operations. Most operations were assigned a name but, as usual, if this one had a name only the company officers knew it. The enlisted Marines went where we were told to go and rarely cared what an operation's name was.

From a mountaintop landing zone, we were helicoptered for about forty minutes to a fairly flat landing area near mountains. It was plain to see that this terrain was hilly and the vegetation was thick jungle surrounded by mountains. For some operations, multiple companies in our battalion would go together, about six hundred and sixty troops. However, this operation only involved our company of one hundred and sixty men.

There is an art form regarding disembarking from a helicopter so you do not break a leg or accidently kill one of your fellow Marines. When helicopters are expecting to take fire during a landing, the pilots want you off the copter as fast as possible and often would not land. Usually, they would hover five to ten feet in the air and the troops jumped as they calculated how high above the ground they actually were.

On this particular landing, some idiot had put a bayonet on his rifle. As he was about to jump, he accidentally dropped his rifle and almost speared a platoon sergeant already on the ground. Rule number one: never, never put a bayonet on your rifle while disembarking from a hovering helicopter.

Our lieutenant informed us that our objective was to "take" a mountain top located about a four-day march away. Everybody was nervous because we all knew that we had landed in a place close to where there were North Vietnamese Army major artillery emplacements. These big 153mm artillery guns would be more than close enough to us to do serious damage. (Fortunately, after a two-day march we had heard nothing from them.) At the end of the second day's march, we settled in amongst thick jungle and tall trees.

This is when a 'minor miracle' occurred.

While we were cutting back brush to create a place to sleep, two helicopters somehow found us and hovered to lower supplies since there was no place for them to land. My squad of about twelve men was getting ready for night activities. These would include such things as assigning and deploying listening posts. These posts often consisted of one or two Marines staying awake in shifts throughout the night. Being surprised by a night attack while on an operation was not a pleasant thought.

While settling in, I was told that there was mail to be distributed. It was unusual in the middle of an operation to receive mail. Nevertheless, mail was always welcomed. My squad leader brought me a package that was fairly large and completely unexpected. What made it even better was that my package arrived on my twentieth birthday. Everybody was telling me to open it! I did and got the surprise of my life – it was a birthday cake!

I found getting a birthday cake from my mom on my birthday in a jungle in Vietnam to be completely unbelievable. I thought to myself that absolutely nobody would ever believe this was happening. In truth, it tasted just as if it had come out of the oven. The postmark indicated it had been shipped from the States nine days previously. I did not cry, but I came close.

My mom was good about sending mail but this was unbelievable! My friends, including Jerry P, another fire team leader, were more than happy to help me eat the cake. None of my friends had ever heard of anyone receiving a birthday cake out here in the jungles of Vietnam. I took some time to silently thank my Mom and

God for such an unexpected experience. The cake was big enough to feed our entire squad. What a day!

After four days of marching, we were getting near our objective. So far, there had been no contact with the North Vietnamese Army. The jungle had gotten so thick that our fire team was picked to take machetes and clear a path to allow the company access. We alternated members of the team so no one person stayed in the lead too long. Even so, it was very slow going and we were all close to exhaustion after about seven hours of cutting.

Around four in the afternoon of the fourth day, we arrived at the base of a mountain surrounded by smaller hills. We were told that military intelligence (using aerial photos) had concluded that the mountain in front of us was thought to be a North Vietnamese Army reconnaissance base. Our photos showed that all paths led to the top of this fair-sized mountain.

Our platoon was sent to climb an adjoining hill to provide cover fire if the other three platoons were ambushed while climbing the mountain. This location was like something out of a movie – a very surreal atmosphere. Fog had started to form around the top of the mountain making seeing anything or anyone at the top impossible.

The assault started promptly on time. The other platoons advanced at a steady pace while we provided cover for them. After about three hours, the climb was completed with no contact. By late afternoon, our platoon joined the company at the summit. On the mountain top was a very large North Vietnamese encampment – there was no doubt that the other side used this place quite often. They had left food, sleeping quarters and clothing. We were quite happy to claim their quarters as our own.

After about thirty minutes of moving in, I remember talking to my friend Jerry about how thirsty I was and he echoed the sentiment. Five minutes later, everything suddenly turned to chaos. Apparently, while we were climbing the front of the mountain, the North Vietnamese were climbing up the backside. We just happened to get to the top first. I remember a sudden long burst of machine gun fire coming from the backside of the mountain. Fortunately, I recognized it as our machine guns and not theirs.

Weeks later, I talked to the men who started the fight on the backside of the mountain. According to my source, one machine gunner from the third platoon had just finished setting his gun up and heard some people laughing and joking as they reached the mountaintop coming from the opposite side. It was a race to see who could fire first.

Fortunately, our men opened up their machine gun first and immediately a short firefight broke out. The North Vietnamese had no idea that we were in their quarters and on their mountain. About ten minutes after the firing ceased our lieutenant called for a fire team to go down the trail and see what the situation was. Obviously, both sides had been caught by surprise.

Technically, it was my team's turn for such a thing, but, because it was my team who had hacked the jungle for seven hours, they skipped my group and picked Jerry's fire team. After fifteen minutes, we had not heard anything. Suddenly there was the sound of a North Vietnamese machine gun. Explosions and more small arms fire followed. Then everything went quiet. The captain sent out another team but there was no contact made. That team however, did bring back the bodies of Jerry and two other Marines.

Apparently, a North Vietnamese machine gun position had caught them with no place to hide. Night was coming fast and intercepted radio traffic was indicating we had stumbled upon the advanced guard of an enemy unit that was at least six times larger than us. Immediately Marine jet fighters were contacted and after about an hour, they dropped 250-pound fragmentation bombs. The jets stayed until they had dropped all ordinance and then returned to base. There was no panic on the mountaintop, but if the radio-intercepted messages of the nearby North Vietnamese troops could be believed, we were vastly outnumbered. Intercepted radio chatter indicated they were going to hit us with everything they had during the night.

We geared up for a major engagement and sat tight

waiting for the show to start. Marines are Marines, but a lot of nineteen and twenty-year-old Marines were sending out many prayers. Battalion headquarters must have been genuinely worried we might be over-run. Somebody very high up the military food chain ordered the aircraft known as "Puff" and "Spooky" to stay on point over our position. One of these special planes would drop high intensity flares that would illuminate anything or anybody under it. The other aircraft could then fire a Gatling gun out of both sides of the airplane. These two were used in critical situations and represented our best bet for surviving the night.

The two planes stayed in the air until two planes identical to them replaced them. In the morning, we were relieved to be alive. The planes had stopped a night attack that could have brought heavy casualties to our company. Intercepted North Vietnamese radio messages indicated that the North Vietnamese somehow thought we were a battalion-sized force on the mountaintop. Between their mistaken size estimate as well as the use of "Puff" and "Spooky" we lived to fight another day. In two days, helicopters came and picked up the company including the dead and wounded.

Author's Note:

This chapter is about two events. The first - having a birthday cake arrive from the States on my birthday and taste like it just came out of the oven. I thought to myself that no one will ever believe this story, but it happened just as described.

The second event was the death of my good friend Jerry under unusual circumstances. It was my team's turn to respond to an engagement with the North Vietnamese. However, since we had spent most of day four chopping limbs and vegetation for the company, the lieutenant sent the next group in rotation. An accident? Luck of the draw? The Hand of God? I do not know but almost fifty years later I still have "survivor's guilt" and nightmares involving that incident.

Why Jerry – why not me? Post-Traumatic Stress Disorder (PTSD) is made of such memories. After all this time I still go in circles mentally trying to understand the Grace of God in this situation.

I have visited Jerry at the "wall" in Washington, D.C. I have gone twice and cried like a five-year old each time. I am left with the age-old question of all warriors – "Why him and not me?" I intellectually do not have an answer and probably never will. However, I still feel deeply that God continues to love Jerry while I still search for unanswerable answers after all these years.

"God have mercy on Jerry and me – Amen."

4
THE "PRESENCE" AND THE LIEUTENANT

"... He Himself has said, I will never leave you nor forsake you." (Hebrews 13:5)

Fall 1968

We were still in the mountains of I-Corps and it was still hot. A new lieutenant had been assigned as platoon leader. He seemed competent enough but generally officers and enlisted men did not mingle. It had taken several months for me to feel accepted by my peers. The reason why is generally because troops who have been "in-country" for several months are slow to warm-up to new additions for a logical reason. Veterans of several or more months in combat are reluctant to "make friends" too quickly. They do not want to get too close to a replacement who may not stay alive more than a couple of weeks. It was a type of emotional self-preservation and it was common throughout the war.

A new staff sergeant was also assigned to our platoon. This guy looked like he had been through multiple wars. He said the Commandant of the Marine Corps had told him to either go back for a third tour of duty in Vietnam or "get out of my Marine Corps". This guy was as laid-back as they came. He did not look or sound as if he would pass an IQ test but he had definitely been "around the block". He had been demoted multiple times for insubordination.

Sergeant R[2] always introduced himself by giving you his name and where he came from – Indiana. He would then proceed to remind you that Indiana was the "Hoosier" state – as in "who's your mama and who's your daddy?" Yes, a bad joke, but he thought it was hilarious and laughed himself to tears.

On a hot day in September, the captain sent our platoon of around thirty marines on a long patrol. All of the company's platoons had been pulling patrol duty at the rate of one every couple of days. So far, we had not made contact so there was no real reason to think that today would be any different. That type of thinking turned out to be a mistake. The new lieutenant and new staff sergeant were in charge of the patrol. The terrain was hilly and footing was not very stable. A little after midday we found ourselves on a long line with the troops separated by a distance of five to six feet. We were walking on a ridge that sat between two opposite mountains.

Around 1:00pm, it "hit the fan". Apparently, the North Vietnamese had been watching our patrols and the routes we tended to follow. While we were walking on a

---

[2] Name Withheld

valley ridge between the two mountainsides, the North Vietnamese pulled the trigger. The "point" men for the patrol were engaged by small-arms fire. This had the effect of stopping the patrol as we spread out and took position to direct small-arms fire to our front. While we deployed to bring fire to our front, the North Vietnamese ambush was initiated.

Across the valley came the sound of heavy mortars being fired. They seemed to know precisely how far away we were because the mortar fire was exactly on target. These were not their small mortars but the large – 81mm mortars, which could propel a large and heavy projectile a long way with great accuracy. As the mortar rounds continued to fall, the ground fire greatly increased. They seemed to have us outnumbered and as the fighting closed in, the machine guns were firing in small bursts to conserve ammunition.

I found myself in a bomb crater with bullets scorching the air around me. The crater provided some shelter from rifle fire but it did nothing to protect me from mortar rounds. I had a clear line of sight to the enemy and was taking advantage of it while I could. I thought that I was lucky to be where I was since I could see them but they could not see me. The mortars from across the valley were beginning to result in us taking casualties. The fighting after forty minutes had turned vicious and extremely loud. Fighting from a distance is not too bad on your ears but close combat is loud beyond imagination.

In the midst of all this, something happened. Suddenly everything around me ceased being so loud. I became very calm and felt a "presence" close by. Everything going on around me looked as if it was in "slow motion". I "heard" a voice tell me to leave my current position immediately! The tone of the "voice" was quiet but insistent.

In human terms, I do not know how to explain what was happening, but the experience was very real and the tone of the voice did not invite any type of discussion. I immediately left my position and moved about thirty yards away. I had been in this new spot for less than ten seconds when the location I had just vacated was destroyed by an 81mm mortar round. Had I remained there, I would have been nothing but a bunch of floating atoms. There was not time to dwell on what had just happened, other than to file the experience away for later as no one would ever believe it.

The fighting went on and our new lieutenant requested jets to fly in and drop bombs on the ambush mortars across the valley. This calmed the mortars down but the ground fighting was becoming vicious. About an hour after the "experience", I found myself in another bomb crater with the new lieutenant, our new staff sergeant and about four other "grunts" like myself. The small-arms fire from machine guns and rifles was deafening and intense. Bullets were kicking up sand all around us. As dire as the circumstances were, this was the time the new staff sergeant decided he needed to relieve his bowels. He acted as if there was nothing to worry about and that he needed to do a "number 2" at the bottom of the crater. Really – you cannot make this stuff up!

The new lieutenant then proceeded to do something I had never heard of before. Regardless of circumstances, he looked every one of us directly in the eyes and apologized for what he was about to do. He said that our group needed to split up and leave our position because where we were was undefendable and one mortar round would kill us all. He actually said he was sorry if his orders got us killed but we could not stay where we were.

I thought this speech was the most impressive thing I had ever heard of regarding an officer and his men. He knew that his order might very likely result in our deaths, so he was apologizing in advance of his order. He indicated which sides of the crater we would exit and wished us good luck.

Before the order could be given, however there was the matter of the new staff sergeant. While the lieutenant had been talking to us, the sergeant was busy looking for toilet paper, which seemed to be in short supply. While this now seems amusing, the lieutenant was not amused and he ordered the sergeant to pull up his trousers. At the count of five, everybody went over the crater top in different directions. To this day, I consider it a miracle that nobody who rolled over the top of the crater was wounded or killed.

Late in the afternoon, the North Vietnamese troops cut off the fight. Our jets had taken out their mortars and without that assistance, they decided to leave the field of battle. We spent the rest of the day calling for medevacs in the form of medical helicopters to pick up the wounded first and the dead later. Our casualties were lighter than I thought and by early evening, the fight was over. We moved back to our base of operations and settled in for the night.

I spent the night thinking about what had transpired during the fight. Remembering "the Presence" gave me a feeling of calmness. I remember the Voice; it had no distinction. It was neither male nor female and as odd as this will read, the Voice was not "heard" in the usual sense. Instead, I felt the Voice rather than heard it. Was this the nearness of an angel?

I was struck by how quiet the Voice was and how clearly I heard the message. It was as if I was the only person there and there was no reason to shout or yell. The authority in the Voice however was nothing to sit around and debate. In fact, if I had not moved immediately I would have died instantly about twenty seconds later.

Did the "Presence" know what choice I would make? To this day, I do not know. All of this was way over my pay grade. Yet, I do know that the Voice on the battlefield was the same Voice I felt during the tiger incident that summer.

5
CLOSE CALL WITH AN M-79

**"You shall not be afraid of the terror by
night, not of the arrow that flies by day..."
(Psalm 91:5)**

Fall 1968

The company was thankfully between operations and we
were encamped close to an artillery platoon. All of us were
occupying a nameless hilltop and were beginning to get used to
the unexpected firing of artillery rounds at odd times – day and
night. Normally, the company was positioned in a defensive
circle designed to provide protection for the artillery platoon.
In order for us to actually get some rest and downtime,
another Marine unit from another battalion had been assigned
to duties of setting up listening posts, patrols and night
ambushes. Although this would not last long, we were quite
happy to get some quality sleep, in spite of erratic artillery fire.

I remember being in a good place mentally. My lieutenant
had told me that the captain had selected me to go to NCO
school in Okinawa the following month. In the Marine Corps,
a non-commissioned officer (NCO) starts at the rank of
corporal. In Vietnam, a corporal could be a fire-team or squad
leader. Platoon commanders were generally low-ranked
officers, such as a First or Second Lieutenant. During my tour
of duty, my platoon leader changed names and faces with
unfortunate regularity.

A platoon officer did not fare much better than an enlisted person when it came to survival. Most of my friends in Vietnam did not worry too much about being killed, but rather, worried about being maimed or crippled. You must realize that most of my fellow Marines were between the ages of eighteen and twenty years old. At those ages, the male testosterone is at its highest. Therefore, rather than dwell on being killed, most of my friends worried about being shot somewhere between the legs. That topic may seem strange but for a nineteen-year-old kid, the topic of certain wounds generated much discussion.

Five days into our down period, an incident took place that I remember with great clarity to this day. The places where most of the enlisted personnel were sleeping really amounted to nothing more than dugout caves. They were each just large enough for one person to crawl into and lie down. Each cave entrance opened to a trench dug around the hilltop. There was much walking activity through the trench so there was not much privacy but none of us really cared. We were just happy to have a place to sleep that was dry and somewhat sheltered. People moving up and down the trench were less than ten feet from me. However, those ten feet were composed of packed earth and had been baked hard by the Vietnam summer so we were content to crawl in and sleep whenever possible.

One afternoon I was in the trench near my cave and was asked by a brand new private fresh from the states to help him clean his personal weapon. In this case, the weapon was a grenade launcher called the M-79. It was a handheld personal weapon that could shoot or launch a fist-sized grenade up to 350 meters. It was a tube in which you placed a 40mm grenade. It took practice to get proficient with it. To be competent with the M-79, you needed to be proficient in estimating yardage between you and the target in front of you. When bullets are flying at you, it takes courage and patience to aim and hit your target. The individuals who carried such weapons could really do some serious damage to the enemy. Such individuals were especially appreciated for their ability to spring North Vietnamese ambushes before they were initiated on the enemy's terms. Shooting or launching an M-79 grenade into a suspected ambush site saved many U.S. lives. One could effectively neutralize the enemy's surprise ambush with one or two grenades launched on their position.

So, this young private asked me for help regarding the cleaning of his weapon. I was a bit put off since I knew he had been taught how to do it. He had only been with the company a week or two and had not been in a fight. He seemed to want to try and do everything right, so I assisted by watching him disassemble any moving parts and cleaning them. The rule when the company was out of "the bush" was that nobody carried around a loaded weapon since some of our own people were killed by an "accidental" discharge of their weapons. After a few minutes observation, I felt it was okay to let him do what he had been trained to do. He continued cleaning in the trench while I crawled back into my narrow cave. About twelve inches of dirt separated the two of us.

In about ten minutes, I heard a sound that took me a second or two to translate into reality. The sound I heard was immediately followed by another sound, that of something hitting the mud ten inches from my head. I popped my head out to see one very frightened private. His face was totally white and his eyes were as wide as saucers. This moron had put a grenade in his launcher and accidentally pulled the trigger. He was staring at a fair-sized hole in the mud right beside me. He had accidentally fired the weapon and it had dug into the trench mud. One of the characteristics of the M-79 was that once the grenade was launched it had to go thirty meters before it was armed and ready to explode. When I poked my head out and saw the mud-hole, everything became crystal clear. As much as I wanted to tear this jerk into pieces, I could not get past what had actually happened.

If that grenade had exploded there would be no me or him. We would have been a pink mist drifting with the air currents. I sent him to the platoon leader while I tried to stop shaking. I had been less than a foot from oblivion. I could actually see the back end of the grenade covered by mud. I immediately felt a calming come over me. I knew that I was not alone and that no harm had been done. I guess one could call what happened "lucky", but I could not help but see the hand of God at work, once again. The young private was severely reprimanded but since nobody had been hurt, the private was sent to a "medic" center in the camp for some tranquilizers to calm him down. He was later sent to another unit and I never saw him again. The memory however has lasted almost fifty years. I can still see his face when I saw what had happened.

Amazing Grace indeed!

6

A HARD NIGHT'S DAY – THE BATTLE OF DaiDo

"A Thousand may fall at your side, and ten thousand at your right hand: but it shall not come near you..." (Psalm 91:2)

I arrived at my company's headquarters on April 14, 1968. After all the months of training, it was somewhat of a relief to reach my company located in the Cua Viet coastal plain of I Corps-Vietnam. My first two weeks quickly taught me immediate lessons in survival. The new life skills, in no particular order, included such things as:

1) When going on a five-hour daytime patrol, always carry four to five water containers so you do not have heat stroke with temperatures over 100°F.

2) Never smoke on a night ambush as the North Vietnamese could smell both you and the smoke and we would be the ones being ambushed.

3) In general, cigarettes were more valued than bullets.

4) If you fell asleep while on a night Listening Post (LP), you ran a real risk of having your throat cut by the other side or "court marshalled" by your own side for

endangering the entire company while they slept.

5) Try to make friends with anybody in your squad who had been "in-country" more than six months. Such people had made a successful transition from civilian to warrior and they were people you could learn from. Unfortunately, the realty was that new troops were on their own for a "break-in" period. Company veterans would not invest emotionally in you since the odds were good that you would not make it beyond a couple of weeks. I know that it sounds "cold" but that was the way it was.

6) Never participate in a night assault with a white towel around your neck.

We spent April 28 getting ready to be helicoptered back to the battalion combat center where we could get hot food and more ammunition. The company officers would meet with other company leaders to coordinate with the battalion's battle plans. The night before had not gone well. We went on a night assault just after dark. Due to some misunderstanding as to where the North Vietnamese were located we actually walked right into a large contingent of North Vietnamese troops – neither side was aware of the proximity of the other. A small skirmish took place leaving several of our people wounded. A disengagement occurred allowing us to request a night medical evacuation by helicopter.

Unknown to us the enemy was the lead unit of a very large North Vietnamese contingent. Around midnight, two copters came for the medical pick-up and unfortunately, their arrival sprung a large ambush from the enemy troops in a semi-circle around our company. Green tracers from three enemy machine guns raked the landing zone. One helicopter was badly shot, but managed to barely skim high enough to fly toward the ocean. It was met by another copter and the wounded on board were flown to the hospital on the USS Iwo Jima positioned just off the coast. I have no doubt that if that copter had crashed in our midst; it would have spurred a full frontal assault against us by a contingent of North Vietnamese larger than our company size force.

We got back early morning of the 28th, promptly took security measures, then fell asleep. That afternoon, our new captain was ordered to leave our current position and bring the company back to the battalion combat center for re-grouping and staging for another operation. Helicopters flew in to pick up our artillery pieces and our supplies. Just about the time we had loaded about a third of our troops to be flown back to the combat center, we started taking artillery fire.

The barrage was so intense and so long in duration that the decision was made to simply walk what was left of the company back to our battalion rear. This proved to be costly. The incoming shells were later estimated to be several hundred shells in a concentrated area. We literally walked through the barrage since it was deemed too dangerous to fly the copters in during a concentrated artillery attack. Somehow, we managed to get to a safer place after about an hour walk. Looking back on it, I cannot believe we actually got back to a safer place at all. Yes, troops were hit but we came out of that walk surprisingly intact.

It did not hurt that after about forty minutes the aircraft known as "Puff" was called in to protect our rear from North Vietnamese forces concentrated behind us. "Puff" had several mini-Gatling guns that could fire from both sides of the plane. It very much discouraged the North Vietnamese from following up behind us.

The next day, April 29, was set aside for the cleaning of weapons, receiving any necessary medical attention and getting as much rest as possible including getting some hot food. Everybody sensed that something big was coming, and we were not wrong. When all your officers spend a lot of time with the battalion commander and his staff, it never leads to something good for the troops.

We woke up early on the morning of the 30th; food was served and weapons checked. Our company walked to a wide river where we halted and were joined by two Marine tanks and two naval landing barges. Each barge was loaded with one Marine tank and two platoons. When we reached the bank of the other side, both tanks and troops disembarked. We spread out and marched at a slow pace as we followed the tanks. In front of us, I could see U.S. Marine fighter planes swooping and dropping bombs and rockets on what looked like a group of villages. We were advancing through rice paddies filled with water so progress was only at a moderate speed. The closer we got to the fighting, the more we could feel the concussions of the bombs exploding 800 meters away. The earth literally trembled and shook after each plane dropped their ordnance. Because this was my first encounter with a real-life military battle, I did not know what to expect, so I prayed to God, not to save me, but to give me the courage to do my duty and not embarrass my family and fellow Marines by being a coward.

We finally walked up to a large section of hedgerows located about 500 meters away from the villages being attacked by the jets. Sitting next to the hedgerows were Marines from another company. They looked tired and disgusted. The battalion's officers gathered for a final check on the battle plan. We were told we would start the assault around 4:00 pm. The Marines already there said they had attacked this section of five villages hours ago and got their butts handed to them. After trying twice, they called in air support and waited for reinforcements and tanks. We were told the fighting in the late morning had been vicious and that the North Vietnamese were well dug in around these villages, one of which was DaiDo. From where I was, I could look past the hedgerows and see that it was about 150 meters of broken terrain to get to the village itself. There were several destroyed pagodas and several dead water buffalo lying in our way. After about a 60-minute wait, the two tanks took position beyond the hedgerows as we waited for orders to advance. Being an assistant gunner for our machine gunner, I had a .45 pistol and some grenades. My job was to carry two cans of ammo and the spare barrel for the machine gun in case the gunner melted down the original barrel, which can happen quickly in a prolonged fight.

My fight started when the two tanks fired point-blank into the pagodas and the village itself. Nothing much happened in terms of a North Vietnamese response. We were then ordered to advance by fire-team rushes (three people per team) as we leap frogged each other to get closer. The North Vietnamese response was almost nothing. We swept through villages and kept advancing until our platoon leader ordered us to halt. We had gotten through and almost nothing had happened.

Another company joined us and we were given orders to go slowly back through the villages. That is when all hell broke loose. Apparently, the North Vietnamese were hoping we would continue walking away while they stayed very well hidden. When they saw us stop and turn around to come back through, they knew that they had not fooled anybody into thinking they had all been killed by the assaults from the planes, tanks, etc. As we turned back through the villages, suddenly the air was choked with bullets flying in all directions. The North Vietnamese had put snipers into some of the trees around the area and they were very effective. At least they were effective, until our Captain directed our M-79 grenadiers to fire point-blank into the trees where the snipers were hiding. This resulted in their neutralization or evacuation. Suddenly, the enemy was everywhere and wanting to fight, but what they really wanted was to get away from that complex of buildings and escape out the far side where there was a vast expanse of buffalo grass; about five feet tall and very thick. It provided good cover to hide in and make an escape.

No matter where my machine gunner went, I was right beside him. We made a good team. Thankfully, he had a lot more experience than I did and he was coolly efficient. He never seemed to be rattled and he fired his weapon efficiently and on-target. The problem with being so close to the gunner was that you quickly realized that you and the gunner drew a lot of attention from the other side. The North Vietnamese were taught to take out our machine gunners as quickly as possible since the machine gun could take down many people in a short time period. Therefore, we drew much attention during the fight. Thankfully, at least on day one, neither of us were hit or compromised by equipment failure.

Darkness ended the first day of fighting. We pulled back about 200 meters from the villages while surrounding them. We dug in and waited. During the night, the battleship USS New Jersey fired its huge artillery rounds for hours at a time. These shells were so large that the ground concussion when they landed would literally rattle your teeth. The ground actually convulsed around us. The shelling took place for several hours. Watching it, I did not see how anybody or anything could survive that kind of beating. Around midnight I was thirsty and sleepy. The old-timers and veterans told us that the North Vietnamese soldiers remaining in the five hamlets would probably try to crawl out through and between our lines. The North Vietnamese knew well what would happen in the morning. At first light we would start to re-engage the enemy. They knew it…and we knew it. Both my gunner and I fell asleep sometime after midnight. I did not sleep well; I kept hearing "pop" noises during the night.

Sometime around 4:00am, I was awakened by a very loud "pop" sound near my head. The new platoon leader, a corporal who had taken over the 2nd platoon after our lieutenant was killed earlier in the afternoon, was standing over me with a smoking pistol in his hand. I looked up at him as he nodded his head in front of me. Ten feet away from us was a very dead North Vietnamese soldier. The corporal said he had been watching this particular enemy soldier as he crawled towards our position for about fifteen minutes. Had our new platoon leader not killed the North Vietnamese soldier, my gunner and I would probably have been killed with a knife as he crawled through our position and our lines.

The company woke early the next morning, the dawning of the second day of a now famous three-day fight against overwhelming odds. It would also be the day I received my first Purple Heart for my first gunshot injury, but that was not until late afternoon.

As we moved again towards the nearest village I saw a Marine sniper who had climbed a few feet up a medium sized tree. He was sighting and firing as fast as he could squeeze the trigger of his telescoped bolt-action rifle. When I looked towards his aiming position, I could see nothing but elephant grass. I asked him what he saw through his scope and he told me I really did not want to know. He finally asked if I had ever heard the expression "... like grains of sand on the beach". I said "no" but got his point. He just looked at me and shook his head.

We slogged through those villages again and managed to sweep through without losing too many men. Around 2:00pm, my gunner took a flesh wound to his right arm. He dropped the machine gun and rolled repeatedly. We were low on ammunition and the gunner could not pick up the heavy machine gun. Just as I was reaching for the gun, I realized someone was standing over me. I looked around and saw the battalion commander Colonel Weise. A cadre of radio people surrounded him. These people stayed in touch with everyone on the ground, ships at sea and the planes flying overhead. He looked down at me and said, "Marine, pick that gun up and start shooting in that direction." He pointed with his index finger to my front. I gave him a big "Aye aye Sir!" Unfortunately for me, the barrel of the machine gun was extremely hot from so much shooting. I was more frightened by the battalion commander than anybody on the other side. Like an idiot, I reached for the weapon, tried to pick it up by the barrel, and promptly melted the flesh of my right hand into the metal itself. I dropped the gun, cursing my stupidity, and not winning any brownie points with the Colonel. Finally, I managed to lift and right the weapon which only had a belt or two of ammunition left. In one of the "highlights" of my thirteen-month stay in Vietnam, I tucked the gun against my right hip and started shooting anything that moved while standing then walking forward. An hour later, my gunner and I lined up with the rest of the battalion creating a long line by a small stream. Across the stream in the high elephant grass were an unbelievable number of enemy troops. Thankfully, we did not know what the odds were at the time.

At a designated time, everyone on our side opened fire with every weapon available. It was an impressive display of firepower and will to fight. About ten minutes later, the other side let loose everything they had as well. Wow, did they ever have so many more troops and firepower. It is always a bad sign of how the fight is going if Marines start putting bayonets on the end of their rifles. My gunner and I set up in the midst of other Marines who had formed a long line of troops split up into small scattered groups of Marines who were out of water and almost out of ammunition. The fighting was getting closer and closer – hand grenades could be seen being thrown by both sides. They were passing each other in the air – heading towards them and coming towards us. It was then that I was hit by an AK-47 round (bullet). One moment I was feeding the last of our ammunition into the gun and in the next second, I was doing a backward flip toward the bottom of a bomb crater. Months later a Marine told me that he was sitting to my left side when I was hit. He said that he thought I was shot through the head because of the backward flip I executed. My first thought when I looked at my left hand was one of resignation; I thought, "There goes my guitar career." I could see the bone of my middle finger on my left hand and the exit wound where the bullet went out through my ring finger. Everything else was just blood flowing quickly. My left hand was numb and felt like I had put my finger into an electric outlet. Ten minutes passed and everything disintegrated into chaos. The corporal who saved my life the night before did it again. He came over to me to check and see how deep a nearby stream was. I checked the depth of the stream and it was only knee-high. The corporal gathered several other platoon troops and said that we needed to leave – "right now". The others I did not know but we ended up with five Marines – all of whom had been hit at least once; some had multiple wounds.

Beyond the stream was chest high elephant grass that stretched for about 200 meters. The battle had become intense and very, very loud. He led us to the high grass and then told everybody to take off their heavy flak jackets and helmets. This was going to be a sprint on our stomachs and excess weight was not needed. Before we separated in the grass, I took a last look at the battle, and wished I hadn't. Knowing that our side was just minutes from being overrun and with little left to fight with, some of the troops were lying on the ground in a catatonic state. Some were crying and some were asking for their mothers. It was a scene from a nightmare that has never left me. Welcome to PTSD.

We spread out enough so we could still see each other but with five to ten yards separating us. Once in position, we crawled on our knees and elbows as fast as possible. About three minutes into our race towards a shot-up pagoda, we suddenly heard the unmistakable sound of bullets clipping the grass around us and flying past our heads. The North Vietnamese had seen our attempt to escape and set up a machine gun on a small hill and started strafing the elephant grass around us. By following the corporal's order to drop our helmets and flak jackets, he had inadvertently saved my life for the third time in less than twenty-four hours. One of the bullets fired in our direction split through the hair on my head. If my helmet had still been on my head, the bullet would either have deflected into my head or possibly blown the helmet off my head and the North Vietnamese would have known exactly where we were. The bullets were literally splitting the air around us. We ignored the bullets and kept on crawling. Then, another miracle happened that saved all our lives.

Earlier in the morning, I had noticed a South Vietnamese spotter plane hovering over the battle. I thought it must have been watching the battle unfold and maybe was directing our artillery to the target. Now, while crawling as fast as we could, I noticed the spotter plane suddenly go into a "dive" mode. The plane was carrying one napalm bomb. The pilot passed so close over our heads that I could see him quite clearly. Next, the bomb exploded right where the North Vietnamese machine gun had been placed. The concussion from the explosion literally lifted us all six inches off the ground. The corporal immediately ordered everyone to get up and run towards the shot-up pagoda ninety meters away. When we reached the pagoda we did not stop but ran as fast as possible for a distant tree line behind which was the Cua Viet River. When we reached the river embankment, nobody even stopped but rather we jumped the twelve feet to the river and started swimming.

We had not been in the river three minutes when a U.S. Navy patrol boat came around a bend in the river and picked us out of the river. I felt saved but not necessarily safe. As the navy personnel were hauling us out of the water, they themselves came under fire. We were put down in the boat's bottom as they opened fire with their twin .50-caliber machine guns. It was very loud and bullets were crisscrossing the land separating the two groups. The exchange did not last long as the naval personnel put their patrol boat in high gear and we headed for the town of Dong Ha. We received medical attention on the boat and were turned over to naval doctors when we disembarked at an aide station in Dong Ha. The doctors attended our wounds and made preparations to have us helio lifted to the floating hospital on the USS Iwo Jima stationed a few miles off shore. My attending corpsman gave me a tetanus shot after cleaning my hand wound. For some reason, the corpsman looked familiar. It turned out that this corpsman was the son of my Presbyterian minister back home in South Carolina. To say we were happy to see each other is a monumental understatement.

I was sent to the hospital ship where I stayed for about five days. The battle of DaiDo would continue for another day making it a three-day fight. Many years after the war, our company's executive officer met with the commanding officer for the North Vietnamese 320th Division and asked him how many troops he had on that three-day fight. His answer was between seven and nine thousand troops. The Second Battalion, Fourth Marines entered the fight with six hundred and sixty-five Marines and came out three days later with one hundred and twenty-five accounted for. The Corps paid a stunning price for those three days. The estimate of enemy losses was between three and four thousand over that three day encounter.

The battle of DaiDo also produced two Congressional Medal of Honor recipients. The captain of "Golf" company (my company) and the captain of "Echo" company. History indicates that it is unusual to have two CMH recipients come out of the same fight. Both recipients now live less than a two-hour drive from me. I have met with both and felt honored to be in their presence.

An interesting side note is that our small group of "crawlers" on that second day of battle were declared to be "missing in action". It took the battalion a long time to be able to account for all of our personnel. In the meantime, my mother received a notice from her congressman that I was listed as MIA. According to my sister, Mother kept it to herself for several days before telling my brother and sister. Later, Mother received a phone call from her congressman saying I had been located and was receiving medical attention on the USS Iwo Jima hospital ship.

All this and I had only been "in country" two weeks with over twelve months left to go. Those twelve months would continue to illustrate "Grace Under Fire".

Author's Note:

Regarding the corporal who saved my life three times in less than twenty-four hours; he was killed by the accidental discharge of his best friend's .45 pistol while it was being cleaned. His death six months after the DaiDo battle and the circumstances of his death have haunted me for almost fifty years.

7
GOODBYE VIETNAM – HELLO PTSD

*"And we know that all things work
together for good to those who love God,
to those who are called according to His
purpose." (Romans 8:28)*

My exit from Vietnam in May of 1969 was as quiet as my entrance. Sometime during the twelfth month of my tour, I was sent from the field and placed in supply in Dong Ha. My platoon leader had not offered an explanation for the transfer but rumor had it that there were some feelings about getting me to a safer area since surely I had used up ten lifetimes of luck. I had mixed feelings about the transfer since I still felt an obligation to men in my squad.

My first stop leaving Vietnam was Okinawa. There the corpsmen worked hard to clean up the "jungle rot" on both my arms. This condition was a skin problem caused by living in the mud during the monsoon season which featured almost daily rain for months. The medical people also checked me out for any re-occurrence of the cellulitis condition that had hospitalized me for a week during month seven of the tour.

Leaving Okinawa, I flew to Hawaii for a short stay and then to San Francisco, California. The flight to San Francisco was comprised of nothing but returning servicemen. I do not remember much about that flight other than apparently the plane flew through a rough storm over the Pacific Ocean. I do remember the plane being tossed around, both up and down, like an elevator on steroids. Fortunately, for the returning troops, multiple bottles of liquor were broken out and passed around soon after the plane lifted off. By the time the storm hit, most of the troops had already passed out. Many of them probably never knew there was a storm.

As we got closer to San Francisco, there was a fair amount of tension beginning to spread among the troops. We had all been told in Okinawa that America had changed a lot during our year visit to Vietnam. Some of the stories told about how Americans had turned against the war and that returning vets were being ill-treated. I could taste the tension in the air as our plane landed. A lot of these troops were just beginning to sober up from the flight, and a lot of these troops were carrying knives strapped to their ankles. They had heard stories about returning vets clashing with war protesters in airports. Although we saw people protesting the war when we arrived, there were fortunately no run-ins of a different type.

In the airport I saw a very pretty young lady who was sitting in a near-by lounge. She did not look as though she had any clothes on from the waist down, so naturally I was curious. Upon reaching her table, I excused my intrusion and politely pointed at her waist and asked her — "What is that called?" She didn't take offense and told me that what she was wearing was called a mini-skirt. I smiled and walked away thinking maybe this is why I was spared in Vietnam. The encounter has never been forgotten and it brings a smile to my face almost fifty years later.

Three weeks later I was honorably discharged and flew from San Francisco to Dallas, Texas and then to Atlanta, Georgia. There I was reunited with my mother, sister and brother. I remember that after the Dai Do experience I sincerely thought that there was no way I would ever see my family again. At that time, with twelve and a half months still left to go, I felt the odds were definitely not in my favor. Fortunately for me, God does not believe in odds and everything that happened to me in Vietnam was with His permission and part of His plan for me. Little did I know then, but His plan encompassed more than those thirteen months in Vietnam. That plan is still unfolding to this day.

The reunion in Atlanta with the family was joyful, nervous and slightly overwhelming. None of us knew what to expect. It had been a long time and David and Becky had grown up a lot. A week later, my sister told ma-ma that the person who returned from Vietnam looked like her brother but that "somebody-else" was living in his body. I tried to calm down and adjust to being safe but that was easier said than done. Even my brother, David, was asking mother, "who is this person living in our home?" Mother, as always, kept her thoughts to herself and tried to pretend that nothing had changed and that everything would turn out fine. For me, I adjusted the best that I could, in spite of the fact that every time the Fire Siren sounded in town to alert the fire department of a fire, I jumped under the bed looking for my helmet and flak jacket. Such incidents left me thinking that I had a long recovery time ahead of me. Well, the recovery time has lasted forty-eight years and counting.

When I returned from Vietnam, there was no such thing as PTSD. Other terms that were sometimes used were "shell shock" or "battle fatigue". PTSD was not recognized officially by the American Psychology Association until 1980. I was officially determined to have PTSD only about six years ago when in my early sixties.

Having spent my professional career as a school psychologist for thirty-five years, I have some thoughts on this matter of PTSD. Being a teacher for over ten years at the Master's Degree level in the area of scientific methodology and statistics, I can try to make my point using a simple formula.

COGNITIVE SHIFT + REALITY PARADOX = SPIRITUAL DEPRESSION

Now let us apply this formula to the reality of real-world combat and maybe a possible explanation of combat related PTSD.

When I first joined my company, as I alluded to in

earlier chapters, I was pretty much ignored. Combat veterans were not going to invest emotionally and be "best buddies" with me or any other newcomers. After being in Vietnam for ten months, I knew what they were waiting for. They were waiting to see if I would make the cognitive shift over the first few months. By this I mean, I had to shift from the reality of nineteen years of living in the U.S. where fistfights were about the only experience I had in combat. The new reality in Vietnam had to be assimilated in order to replace the old reality of life in the U.S. This was a new reality where people didn't die; they were killed, and the assimilation process had to happen very quickly. People's deaths, possibly even my own, could be quick or agonizingly slow and painful beyond comprehension. Another new reality was that battlefields are incredibly loud, always confusing, and stink to high heaven. You can always find a recent battlefield using only your nose. Only after accepting this new reality of quick death, loneliness, uncertain future and life measured in twenty-four hour increments, were you then accepted by the combat veterans.

Having made the cognitive shift to increase my chances of survival, I now entered the reality paradox. This new paradox basically states that the new skills you have learned in order to survive are the same skills that will work against you when, and if, you survive your tour and rotate back to the U.S. In Vietnam, a new trooper had to learn certain survival skills. One was that you never bunched up when the fighting started. This goes "directly against" the human desire to share your anxiety with your new friends. I was told a hundred times that if we bunched up, then only one hand grenade was needed to take out multiple troops rather than a single individual. So the paradox begins and shows up in PTSD as a need for isolation and fear of crowds and crowded places, like shopping malls. The Marine Corps is built on the idea of individuals operating effectively within a small group. This concept works very well in close combat situations which is what Marines are famous for. A simple statement of fact is that Marines will fight anybody, anywhere, at any time. In my nineteen months with the Corps, I only once knew of one person who tried to run away to the U.S. while on R&R (rest and relaxation). This individual took a plane from Hawaii to his hometown of Chicago. The FBI arrested him and he was sent back to Vietnam to join his unit, my unit. When he finally arrived back to join the company, he had the crap beat out of him late one night. He was soon more afraid of his platoon members than of the North Vietnamese. We never had another problem with him.

Another paradox effect was that on watch or listening post, two people depended on each other to literally watch each other's back so nobody crawled up and slit your throat. Those same two people back in the states will unconsciously go into a bar and sit with their backs to the wall so they can watch people in front of them and nobody can come up behind them. These are part of the survival skills learned overseas that do not translate back in the States. Another part of the paradox would be the exaggerated sense of hyper-vigilance. This was a needed skill in Vietnam but this same skill does not work well back home. In other words, the survival skills needed in combat simply aren't accepted back in the States. Back home in the U.S., the person you became in Vietnam is not necessarily accepted very well by friends or family. Your family and friends may find you difficult to be around and don't understand why you are so different from the person they grew up with or hung out with just two years ago.

So, when you add cognitive shift to reality paradox it seems to end up as PTSD which is considered a trauma disorder and is routinely treated by medications along with group and individual counseling, e.g. cognitive therapy. Having been in group counseling for the last six years, I can honestly state that the medication and counseling are useful to relieve some of the high anxiety common among returning veterans. However, I can't say that I have seen anybody cured or healed. The VA counselors I have worked with were and are very good at what they do. The best counselors have learned the way to get the members of counseling groups to help heal each other. I've seen that work quite effectively. It wasn't a cure but it did relieve some of the anxiety common among PTSD vets. A common complaint in the group is that these vets not only live in a state of high anxiety but they have trouble making new friends. Their social avoidance makes long-term marriages a low-frequency behavior.

We end up with a concept I refer to as spiritual depression. This term is not originally mine but was first proposed by the British theologian and medical doctor, Dr. Martyn Lloyd-Jones. His book "Spiritual Depression: Its Causes and Its Cure" was published in 1965. The book was not written specifically with PTSD in mind but is useful to re-direct the anxiety and hyper-vigilance to turning the problems of these vets over to the Great Healer – God.

8

CHASING THE WHITE RABBIT – THE POWER OF DENIAL

*"The mind of man plans his way, but the
Lord directs His steps" (Proverbs 16:9)*

I came home in May of 1969. Initially, I did not feel very different although I had been away from family and friends for nineteen months and thirteen days. Coming home from Vietnam, I made a vow to myself to forget about the war experience and get on with my life. Just pick up life where you left it nineteen months ago. I wanted normalcy – I wanted my old life back. I was determined to pick up my old life and forget about Vietnam and all the dream/nightmares that began soon after I tried to recover my life.

It would take decades to realize that the world had not changed but I had. Any thoughts that hinted that it was I who had changed were quickly rejected and denied. Where was God during this time? Where He had always been – right beside me. However, God had given humankind "free will" from the beginning and He would not intervene until I was ready. I am sure that both God and my friends would confirm that I can sometimes be a "little" stubborn. God would not intervene until I was really ready for His assistance. It is amazing to me now that I had fundamentally changed. Changed for the "better" or "worse"? There was no way to answer that question during that 1969 timeline. While I was blinded to my real situation, friends and family saw the personality changes almost immediately but did not know how to bring the subject up. So they kept silent.

What were they seeing that I couldn't or wouldn't see? There seems to be a litany of behaviors that were noticeable to certain people. Primary among the changes were things like aloofness, a "thousand yard" stare, distractibility, difficulty with repressed anger, and not going to crowded places like malls or any place where many people gather. What others could not see was something that I could not shake – "survivor's guilt". I was haunted by thoughts of all my friends whose deaths I had witnessed. Especially Jerry P (mentioned in an earlier chapter). It had been my squad's turn to react to a confrontation with the North Vietnamese yet we were passed over and Jerry's squad went down that trail and within 5 minutes, Jerry and two others in his patrol were killed. Such situations are next to impossible to reconcile.

Why him and not me? My sister, as usual, maybe had the best hypothesis. She said that I was meant to write my story in hopes that maybe others in my boat might find some hope from it. Whether this manuscript is published or not, it has already changed the dynamics of my relationships with my son and my daughter. Vietnam was never discussed with them – I thought I was sheltering them from a subject difficult to express. That was a mistake. They had a right to know, but I did not want to contaminate them with the horrors of war. This story has definitely changed my son's perspective of what his "old man" did in the war.

My son was our first-born and was named Lee. Lee is not a family name. We decided upon it because he was born several days before his "due" date on Robert E. Lee's birthday. I had always been a strong admirer of Robert E. Lee mainly due to his characteristics of strong religious faith and his humility in all circumstances. My son has grown up to be a musical prodigy and is a damn nice human being.

If you have not discussed your war experience when your kids are old enough to understand – you are making a big mistake. Your kids will understand what you have dealt with in silence for years and they will understand and love you more than you would ever predict.

My first summer back, 1969, contained some interesting events – Woodstock and the landing on the moon come to mind. In the fall of 1969, I enrolled in Erskine College, a small church-affiliated liberal arts college. My major was psychology. My sister and brother were attending the same college. I had already attended about a year and a half of college at the University of South Carolina, prior to entering the Marine Corps, and with those credits I was a student at the college for about two and half years. Most of the male students were worried about the military draft that was one worry I did not share with my classmates.

Since some biblical classes were required, I talked to some of the theology professors about what they thought God's feelings were regarding killing and war. They seemed to have mixed opinions regarding the topic – "Is there a difference between killing and as an act of murder?" I doubt God approves of war but if you read of the constant fighting as it occurs in the Old Testament – God is surely familiar with the concept and activity of war.

At school, I made some friends and enjoyed the proximity of seeing my sister and brother on a fairly regular basis. I was still in denial that the war experience had changed me. I had only one clash regarding the war. It occurred at an assembly meeting where all the students met in a large auditorium once a month. The assembly started with a prayer followed by whatever program activities the school officials wanted to present and discuss. On this particular day, the prayer was conducted by a longhaired young man who petitioned God to forgive us for being in Vietnam and for all the destruction our country had brought to that country. I made sure that the school officials knew how I felt about the inappropriateness of the prayer. I made my point without anybody getting hurt. However, that prayer really ticked me off and I made my point of view very clear.

I graduated with a Bachelor of Arts degree in the field of Psychology and immediately got a job close to the town where my mother lived. I worked as a psychological counselor at a regional center for the Developmentally Disabled. I commuted from home to my workplace about twenty miles away. Mom never brought up the subject of Vietnam although she knew that I was hiding the pain of bad memories, bad dreams, guilt and unexpressed anger. The anger was a genuine problem, which kept boiling and seeking an outlet. I was not on any medications and probably should have been.

I never discussed my involvement in Vietnam to anybody. If asked about my military service, I simply said that I was in the military and was in Vietnam and that was the end of the conversation. To me, what happened in Vietnam was not a topic for casual conversation. I would not have been able to explain war and my involvement with it. To be truthful, the person asking about Vietnam really did not want to know what happened and would not have understood my experience. It was easier simply to change the subject without being rude. Surprisingly, my uncles and cousins sometimes inquired about the war but they never pushed me about my experiences and I did not encourage a lot of discussion.

Although I knew I was not doing well in my adjustment to civilian life, only my immediate family could see the struggle for normalcy. I seemed to bounce between introversion and extroversion. The dreams continued and it was not uncommon to wake up with a soaked bed from tears and sweat. In the dreams, I could hear the screams and smell the blood. Even if I had wanted counseling, it would not be readily available. During this time, there was no disorder called Post-Traumatic Stress Disorder and the idea of going for counseling was an admission of personal weakness. In my mind, I just felt that I needed to "toughen up" and these problems would "go away". It was during this time that I decided that the way to handle this problem was to "pass for normal" at work and then sometimes "fall apart" at night. I followed that pattern until I retired in 2009.

One good thing happened during this period. I took a girl to Charleston, South Carolina for a party that my sister was involved in. At that party, I saw and met a really pretty girl who was originally from the Myrtle Beach area. She was teaching music in the Charleston public schools. I had my sister get her name and address. A couple of weeks later, I went to Charleston to date her and within six to eight months, we were engaged. While I was still in denial regarding my adjustment or non-adjustment to "normal" life, I was entering one of the happier times of my life.

9
JUST UNDER THE SURFACE

*"Therefore, my beloved brethren, let every
man be swift to hear, slow to speak, slow
to wrath; for the wrath of man does not
produce the righteousness of God"
(James 1:19-20)*

The girl that caught my eye at the Charleston party became my wife in a six to eight month window. She was cute and musically gifted with a steady job in the local school district. We lived for a short period in western South Carolina before I was accepted for graduate study in psychology at a university in the mountains of western North Carolina. I finished my degree in about two and a half years and we moved back to western South Carolina for year before moving to eastern Iowa.

The state of Iowa had significantly re-written its regulations and policies regarding special needs students and had divided the state into Area Education Agencies (AEAs). I interviewed for a position in the Davenport area and got it. With my wife very much pregnant with our first child, we left the South and began life in the mid-west. Our time in Iowa lasted about four to five years. It was probably my happiest time since leaving Vietnam but cracks were already beginning to reveal the stress and pressure points were building.

We returned to coastal South Carolina and got positions with the local school district. My wife knew of my involvement in Vietnam but not much else. All during these years the topic of Vietnam and what happened there rarely, if ever, was discussed. I never brought it up for discussion and neither did my wife. Every once in a blue moon the topic might arise with a simple question like – "were you in the war?" I would usually indicate that I had been in the war but that was pretty much where the discussion stopped. I simply saw no reason to re-live that thirteen-month period when the person I was talking to could not understand. After all, to talk about it, was to re-live those experiences when I had no desire to analyze that portion of my life. I felt "lucky" to have survived the war and saw no reason to talk about it either with my wife or with anyone else.

For better or worse, the best VA counselors that I have watched are able to divide your experiences in Vietnam into two categories – what happened to you during your stay and what you did during your stay. The best counselors seem to be able to move from "what happened to you" to "what you did". It seems that if you can make that transition as a counselor – then the healing is possible. In other words, any secrets that can be brought out under the question "what did you do" seem to promote communication that is more concise and to release the demons that play with your mind.

After being back in South Carolina for about two

years, our second child, a girl, was born. She was named Rebekah and was absolutely gorgeous. She is in her early thirties now with a beautiful six year old daughter of her own. My kids and grandchild have helped me back to a new normalcy.

In the early 1980s, things began to unwind. One particular incident took place on a golf course of all places. I had taken up the game when I was in graduate school and truly loved it.

On a Saturday, I was playing with three friends who I knew well and enjoyed their company. After playing the first few holes, I faintly heard some "popping" sounds. Something inside me began to stir. I continued to hear the "pops" as our group made the turn after playing the first nine holes. After we stopped for a snack, we started on hole 10. The "pop" sounds were now very close and I knew what the sounds were – a small caliber rifle was being fired from one of the homes located above the course. It was being fired down toward a small creek adjacent to the course. I grew increasingly nervous and angry. In the middle of the tenth hole, I heard a bullet fly past my head. Apparently, the shooter (who I assumed was a young male) did not realize that bullets flying at a high rate of speed will skip off the surface of water depending on the angle. I absolutely lost it! I threw my golf club down and starting screaming as loud as possible.

My friends were just now realizing what was happening. To this day, I think they were more afraid of me than the shooter. I moved as close as I could to the creek and screamed up to the shooter. In no uncertain terms, I screamed that if he fired one more shot I was coming up the hill and would stuff his rifle up his butt. I was so angry that I was trembling all over. After two minutes of trembling and very sure of what I would do if another shot was fired – nothing happened. No shooting and no conversation.

Eventually, we moved on and finished our round of golf. I was shaken to the core. It had been fifteen years since Vietnam yet I had been instantly transported to a land far away. Emotionally, it took me weeks to come down from that emotional ambush I had experienced. In one short experience on a golf course, I had all the demons revisit me. I could not believe that all those combat experiences had been hiding just under the surface. Even more unsettling was what I had been willing to do if the shooter fired another shot. I knew that I would have hurt somebody very badly. It was miserable to know that I might have left Vietnam but my experiences in Vietnam had not left me.

I now felt very vulnerable and bouts of depression soon followed. I went to a licensed psychiatrist who diagnosed me as having a condition named dysphoria – a mild precedent to depression. The doctor did not seem to want to explore the Vietnam experience. He seemed to want to discuss my family history. I found that unusual as there was no history of depression running in my family. He eventually put me on Lithium. It brought some relief but I knew the medicine was not going to cure the emotions running out of control just under my skin.

On the domestic front, everything was nearly perfect. I had a great family and we were financially secure. I played the role of a successful professional during the day and did what I had to in order to be the thoughtful husband and proud father of my two kids. Then I threw it all away.

I met a female educator at a conference. She lived in another state, and at first there were no fireworks. She was pretty and very smart. I ran into her again a few months later at a national conference on the west coast. Why? With everything going for me, would I jeopardize everything I had worked for? I wish I could answer that question. Over a period of ten months, I moved out of my home and got an apartment. Next came a divorce and five months later another marriage.

At first things worked fine but within three years the new wife decided she wanted to leave and move back to her home state. Next thing I knew, I was getting a divorce notice by mail. As bad as my personal life was, my professional career was somehow getter better and better.

After about ten years there was one more attempt at marriage. This one lasted about three years and after that I swore off marriage. It had become obvious that for whatever reason I was not cut out for long-term relationships. Over the years I have reconciled with my children and have stayed close to them.

10
DANCING WITH THE VA

"Hope deferred makes the heart sick, but
when the desire comes, it is a tree of life"
(Proverbs 13:12)

From 1969 to 2009, I had almost no involvement with the Veterans Administration. The only two exceptions were the student loans for my graduate school study and a home loan for my first house. I was still in total denial that my involvement in the Vietnam War had left me badly damaged as a functioning human being. This state of denial was not evident to other persons I met and worked with. Somehow, I was able to have a successful career but my private life was a disaster. I spent so much energy trying to pass for 'normal' that my private life was a time to recoup what energy was left – and it was not much. The nightmares and crying jags simply would not go away – and the medication only helped in terms of getting some sleep.

My active VA involvement started in September of 2009. Once my service in Vietnam was validated by my records, I was allowed to join a local counseling group located about twenty miles from my home. I went once a week. The person running the group was a combat veteran as well as a being a local minister.

The VA system was initially very confusing. It was difficult to distinguish between where counseling services were offered, medical services were offered, and where the county VA offices were located and what services were offered there.

Initially, the counseling services were group services and my group was large – too large. I attended and mostly listened to others' stories. The one thing I learned, that was useful, was that many of the veterans in my group had identical symptoms as myself.

The VA assigned me a 50% disability rating based on Compensation and Pension (C&P) interviews held in Charleston, South Carolina. In addition to my 50% disability, I was also assigned a 10% rating for tinnitus – constant or intermittent buzzing in one or both ears.

After three years, our VA counseling group was split up because it had become too large. I was assigned to a small, all-combat-only group. The actual number of veterans who had actually pulled the trigger turned out to be very small. The assigned counselor turned out to be very good and very professional. He took time with me on an individual basis and gave me the encouragement to continue attending the counseling sessions (weekly). He also helped me run the bureaucratic maze in trying to get a higher disability rating.

The problem with going to C&P interviews was

that there was no continuity among the people interviewing you. Some interviews lasted thirty minutes and one, in Charleston, lasted two hours and fifteen minutes. In general, it took between six to nine months to get a response back. As of this writing, I find myself in the same situation again. As of this morning, I was told that it would probably take a year before the Dispute Review officer (DRO) would make a decision regarding my eligibility for 100% disability status.

This delay in responding to veterans, especially those who are older, is a major sore point with veterans. Older veterans from wars like Vietnam are chronologically running out of time. Many older veterans feel strongly that the VA has adopted a practice of "hurry up and wait" regarding responding to older veterans. VA responses of a year or more are intolerable and the message sent from the VA to the veteran is interpreted as "hurry up and die". This may seem harsh to many but to veterans who were wounded multiple times in close combat, fighting for our country, the time delays for VA decision-making is ridiculously slow or maybe even deliberately slow. With the current veteran suicide rate of over twenty deaths a day, much could be improved.

11
PTSD AND COUNSELING

"It is better to trust in the Lord than to put confidence in man" (Psalm 118:8)

To alleviate the symptoms of PTSD, the VA offers two avenues of assistance. One is counseling, either group or individual or a combination of both, and the other is the dispensing of pharmaceutical medicines – usually to aid with sleeping and depression. Both depression and the inability to stay asleep are quite common symptoms of PTSD.

I have been attending VA counseling sessions – sometimes once a week and sometimes every two weeks – for five years now. One of the best things to happen for veterans like myself occurred in 1980. At that time, the American Psychological Association (APA) added PTSD to the 3rd Edition of its Diagnostic & Statistical Manual of Mental Disorders (DSM-III). This was a significant step because 1) it acknowledged that PTSD was "real" and 2) the APA insisted that PTSD was not caused by some genetic or personality deficiency but rather the causal agent for PTSD was "outside" the individual – not a personality deficiency but a causal agent like trauma from being in a combat zone for thirteen months. No longer will combat veterans be shamefully referred to as "shell-shocked" or "battle fatigued".

Having a Master's Degree in Psychology, I have experience with counseling; I know when counseling is effective and when it isn't. My current group has about six to seven individuals who were combat vets from the Vietnam era. Our group is comprised of both Blacks and Whites, both enlisted and military officers. Our assigned counselor is an ex-Army enlistee and served in the sands of Saudi Arabia. I can honestly say that I have not seen any of my counseling group get "cured" from PTSD. However, I have seen individuals begin making better life decisions. Decisions that helped the vet and not decisions that hurt them. In my opinion, smaller groups are more effective than large groups. I am fortunate to have an effective counselor. A small group of vets will open-up if-and only if-they feel "safe" in their counseling group. That "safe" environment takes time to establish.

In my opinion, conditions that promote "PTSD" symptoms can fall into two categories. 1) Things that happened <u>to</u> you in Vietnam, and 2) things that <u>you</u> did in Vietnam. If a counseling group can open-up and discuss the first of these – "What happened to you?" then the VA counselor has a right to feel that progress is being made. I have witnessed group conversation regarding "what happened to you", but I have never heard a confession or discussion regarding "what you did in Vietnam". Maybe the second category would be more appropriate in individual counseling. My experience in Vietnam would indicate that if a counselor could get the veteran to share some things he was forced to do to stay alive – possible healing might come more quickly. Most combat veterans do not want to re-live certain acts they were forced to do to stay alive. Therefore, the traumas continue to interrupt their lives. These veterans might be looked upon as being traumatized. Another term that might be more appropriate would be that these vets are "spiritually depressed". The term introduced by Dr. Lloyd-Jones. I don't know why but that term "spiritually depressed" has always struck close to home. It seems to ring a personal bell with me.

I'm often asked, "So where is God in all of this"? My answer is always that God is where He has always been – right beside you. Should he be busy, He has lots of angels ready to do His bidding. I've bumped into a few of them along life's journey. I also ran into a few of them in Vietnam.

I don't see PTSD as some sort of disease. Rather, in my case, fighting PTSD has opened doors and avenues of personal development that would never have happened otherwise. It may seem like a big price to pay but I know that I'm better as a person because of what I have had to learn about myself and the mysterious way God works.

--Amen.

A final thought regarding PTSD –

The Bible says "God is love." Therefore, my resolution is:

1. Find somebody to love;
2. Love what I do; and
3. Have something to look forward to.

-Adapted from the writings of George Washington Burnap
(1848)

AFTERWORD
A PASTOR'S PERSPECTIVE ON PTSD
By Rev. Randy Riddle

"Come to Me, all you who labor and are
heavy laden, and I will give you rest."
(Matthew 11:28)

It is a wonderful privilege for me to offer helpful information to my fellow veterans and especially to those combat veterans like my good friend, Ben, whose Vietnam experience as a combat Marine and the years following are described in this personal account of "Grace Under Fire". So before going further, let me first introduce myself, giving you some idea of who I am and why I may be of help to other combat veterans like Ben.

I am a 75-year-old college-educated, seminary-trained, Presbyterian minister, with over 55 years' life experience as a member of America's armed forces (USAF, with both overseas and stateside duty stations), as a corporate marketing employee (Humble Oil & Refining Co., now Exxon-Mobil), and as the pastor-teacher for three local church congregations. A life-changing turning point occurred in my life as a 30-year-old oil company marketing representative when, for the first time, I came to understand the power of the Gospel of Jesus Christ to change lives. I came to understand that before my Creator God, despite my best efforts to change my self-centered and self-destructive habits and lifestyle, I was unable to do so. The reason, as I learned later, was because I was *"...dead in trespasses and sins" (Ephesians 2:1.* But for reasons that I have yet to understand, God made me alive together with Jesus Christ by His grace *(Ephesians 2:4-5)*, not only changing my life from one of sinfulness selfishness to God-centered righteousness, but also giving me a purpose for living. Since that life-changing experience over 45 years ago, I have sought to thank Almighty God for His work of grace in my life by seeking to faithfully serve Him and my fellow humans. So, over these many years now, God and His written word, the Bible, have been my infallible guide, sustainer and source of comfort through the ups and downs of married life, family life, pastoral ministry, in ill health and good health, in the good times and bad times and especially so in the increasingly uncertain times in which we now find ourselves. I have been privileged to discover the truth of *Psalm 118:8*, which states, *"It is better to trust in the Lord than to put confidence in man."*

By trusting in the Lord as He has made Himself known in His written Word, the Bible, I have had an anchor for my soul through life's many storms.

So the main point I want to make with my

introduction is this: I believe that unless someone has a medically-diagnosed physical problem, God's Word gives hope that a non-medically-diagnosed problem has a spiritual solution. In other words, the perspective and counsel I offer for PTSD in the remainder of this afterword to **"Grace Under Fire"** is spiritual, not psychological, nor medical. I am a Christian pastor, not a psychologist, nor psychiatrist, nor medical doctor.

Now that I have given you the reader a better idea of just who I am and my qualifications for writing this concluding portion of **"Grace Under Fire"**, let me address the problem of PTSD from three perspectives:

- a Biblical and pastoral perspective

- a Biblical, pastoral and medical perspective of medically-trained physician and long-serving minister of the historic Westminster Chapel in London, Dr. D. Martyn Lloyd-Jones

- the World War II combat veteran and prisoner of war, Olympic track star Louis Zamperini

First, in order to accurately understand the root cause of the problem, along with its many symptoms, it would be wise to understand, as I have for many years, that *"it is better to trust in the Lord than to have confidence in man" (Psalm 118:8)*. While all 66 books of the Bible illustrate this truth, none is better for God's spiritual diagnosis of PTSD, God's remedy for PTSD, and gratitude for a PTSD-free life than the *New Testament book of Romans.* This book is especially important because it can be divided into three easily-distinguishable parts that address every aspect of the problem from a spiritual perspective:

- **Guilt (1:18-3:20);**
- **Grace (3:21-11:36);** and
- **Gratitude (12:1-16:27).**

The theme or central truth of **Romans** is stated in **chapter one, verses 16-17:**

> *"For I am not ashamed of the gospel of Christ, for it is the power of God to salvation for everyone who believes, for the Jew first and also for the Greek. For in it the righteousness of God is revealed from faith to faith; as it is written, 'The just shall live by faith.'"*

In other words, **the power of the Gospel of Jesus Christ changes lives!** That's God's ultimate solution to man's universal problem of *Guilt,* which He begins to describe in *chapter one, verse 18,* and continues on through *chapter three, verse 20.* The problem is our sin – our failure to meet God's righteous standard through our human efforts. He puts it in these words in *chapter three, verses 10-12:*

*"There is none righteous, no, not one;
there is none who understands; there is
none who seeks after God.
They have all gone out of the way;
They have together become
unprofitable;
there is none who does good, no, not
one."*

God is telling each and every one of us that our problem
is sin – that we all fall short of His righteous, moral
standards, summarized in His **Ten Commandments
(Exodus 20:1-17 and Deuteronomy 5:6-21)**. We stand
guilty before Him and this is every man's natural
condition even if we never experience the violence and
trauma of physical warfare. So when the physical and
psychological effects of combat are added to the
symptoms of man's already-existing sinful nature, the
effects become obvious and pronounced, as described by
Korean War veteran Al Rasmussen **("P.T.S.D.
Symptoms," "The Chosin Few", April-June 2011)**:

**"Recurrent, intrusive, and distressing
thoughts about the event. Recurrent
dreams, nightmares (sometimes called
'night terrors') about the event.
Flashbacks (a sense of reliving the**

event). **Distress, caused by reminders of the event (sights, sounds, smells). Alienation, isolation and avoidance of people and places. Emotional numbing. Survivor guilt (for having survived when others did not, or for behavior required for survival). Difficulty falling asleep or staying asleep. Anger and rage. Difficulty concentrating or remembering certain facts about the event. Hypervigilance, or survivalist behavior even after you are away from the event. Exaggerated startle responses (usually to loud noises)."**

Thus, according to the Bible, there are, and always have been, two kinds of warriors in any combat situation. There are those, like Ben, who take with them on the battlefield a measure of God's grace that may protect and preserve their lives, enabling them to possess an unlimited spiritual reservoir from which they can draw as they deal with the horrors of combat and the subsequent symptoms of PTSD. For them, there is always hope outside of themselves. Then there are those whose only reservoir to deal with the same circumstances is what they carry with them into battle. They possess only their own human resources, which are finite and limited. So it is not surprising at all that those who possess a sinful nature and a life scarred by war's trauma would lead to a destructive lifestyle. To some of these, the only hope they have is the VA counseling and prescribed pharmaceuticals to suppress their PTSD symptoms, which far too often, is not enough, with some resorting to suicide as their only hope for ending their suffering.

Thankfully, there is hope for a life-changing solution to this problem that addresses not just the symptoms, but the root cause of the problem. This is the *second part of Romans: Grace (3:21-11:36)*. In this part, God explains His solution in terms of His free grace through faith alone in Jesus Christ alone. He writes in *Romans 10:9-10*:

> *"...If you confess with your mouth the Lord Jesus and believe in your heart that God has raised Him from the dead, you will be saved. For with the heart one believes to righteousness, and with the mouth confession is made to salvation."*

Jesus Himself explains God's solution to man's sinful nature and the trauma of PTSD with this invitation as recorded by the Gospel writer, Matthew:

> *"Come to Me, all you who labor and are heavy laden, and I will give you rest. Take My yoke upon you and learn from Me, for I am gentle and*

lowly in hear, and you will find rest for your souls. For My yoke is easy and My burden is light" (Matthew 11:28-30).

The third and final part of **Romans** is one of **Gratitude (12:1-16:27)**; that is, how God says the one who is the recipient of His free grace and deliverance from sin and the ravages of PTSD is to demonstrate their gratitude. This, then, is the solution from a Biblical and pastoral perspective.

Added to this Biblical and pastoral perspective is a medical perspective by medically-trained physician, Dr. D. Martyn Lloyd-Jones, and long-serving minister of the historic Westminster Chapel in London. Two of his published works confirm this perspective.

Spiritual Depression – Its Causes and Cure (Wm. B. Eerdmans Publishing Company, Grand Rapids, Michigan 1965), and

Exposition of Romans (The Banner of Truth Trust, Edinburgh, UK 2000). The first three volumes that cover **1:1-4:25** are fundamentally important because they explain in detail our **Guilt** and God's **Grace** alone through faith alone in Jesus Christ alone. The 12th volume explains the resulting **Gratitude** of the redeemed sinner (i.e., "Christian Conduct").

A one volume edition by another reliable Bible scholar, Dr. R. C. Sproul, though not a medical physician, explains the meaning and applications of Romans in the same manner as Dr. Lloyd-Jones. This volume is titled, "The Gospel of God – An Exposition of Romans (Christian Focus Publications, Great Britain 1999).

A third and final perspective is one of the clearest and best illustrations of the power of the Gospel of Jesus Christ to deliver a combat veteran ravaged by PTSD is the life of Louis Zamperini. Zamperini was an Olympic track star who survived his World War II bomber crash into the Pacific Ocean, adrift in a life raft for 47 days, only to be captured and tortured by the Japanese for more than two years. He wrote that after he came home at the end of WWII, he had all the classic symptoms of PTSD, until He discovered God's solution to his problems. A young Christian evangelist, Billy Graham, was preaching the life-changing Gospel of Jesus Christ in a 1949 crusade in Los Angeles. It was during that crusade that Zamperini's life was dramatically changed, his PTSD symptoms disappeared and the remainder of his life was one that demonstrated a deep gratitude to his Creator and Redeemer God for delivering him from his sin and misery of PTSD. His remarkable story has been written about in Laura Hillenbrand's **"Unbroken – A World War II Story of Survival, Resilience, and Redemption";** **"Don't Give Up, Don't Give In – Lessons from an Extraordinary Life"** by Louis Zamperini & David Resin; and a Billy Graham Evangelistic Association DVD,

"Captured by Grace".

Finally, I conclude my pastoral counsel by saying to each and every combat veteran suffering from the symptoms of PTSD: There is **<u>HOPE</u>** for a lasting solution to your problem. It is found in the written *Word of God, the Bible,* and specifically, in the *New Testament book of Romans,* where you can come to understand and, by God's grace, experience:

Our **GUILT** as a sinner before Almighty God, justly deserving God's displeasure and your misery;

God's free **GRACE** alone through faith alone in Jesus Christ alone as the only means of delivering you from your sin and misery; and

Our **GRATITUDE** for God's deliverance enabling you to live a PTSD-free life.

> *"Oh, the depth of the riches both of the wisdom and knowledge of God! How unsearchable are His judgments and His ways past finding out!*
> *'For who has known the mind of the Lord?*
> *Or who has become His counselor?*
> *Or who has first given to Him and it shall be repaid to him?'*
> *For of Him and through Him and to Him are all things, to whom be glory forever. Amen"*
> *(Romans 11:33-36).*

References

Lloyd-Jones, D. M. (1965). Spiritual Depression: Its Causes and Its Cure. Grand Rapid, Michigan: Eeardmans Printing Company.

Nolan, K. (1994). The Magnificent Bastards: The Joint Army-Marine Defense of Dong Ha, 1968. New York: Presidio Press.

Sledge, E. (1981). With the Old Breed: At Peleliu and Okinawa. California: Presido Press.

About the Author

Ben Barbour (pictured above left) is a two time recipient of the Purple Heart for his service as a combat Marine in the Vietnam War where he served as a front-line rifleman and machine gunner. He is a retired school psychologist with 29 years of experience in educational positions in Iowa, North Carolina, and South Carolina. Drawing from his personal experience with Post-Traumatic Stress Disorder and his professional training and experience, he has lectured extensively on behavior disorders. His experiences in combat and his struggle with PTSD were instrumental in his professing Jesus Christ as Lord and Savior. He is now retired and lives in South Carolina.

Rev. Randy Riddle (pictured above right) is Ben's minister and served as the motivation for the ultimate writing of this book. Also a military veteran, Rev. Riddle provides counseling and insight into the unique traumas that confront our veterans returning to the home front.

For more information, please visit our website at www.bbarbourgrace.com.

CPSIA information can be obtained
at www.ICGtesting.com
Printed in the USA
LVOW01s2111181216
517871LV00018B/1046/P